POEMS
OF LONG AGO

by Roy H Stoller

DORRANCE
PUBLISHING CO
EST. 1920
PITTSBURGH, PENNSYLVANIA 15238

The contents of this work, including, but not limited to, the accuracy of events, people, and places depicted; opinions expressed; permission to use previously published materials included; and any advice given or actions advocated are solely the responsibility of the author, who assumes all liability for said work and indemnifies the publisher against any claims stemming from publication of the work.

All Rights Reserved
Copyright © 2023 by Roy H Stoller

No part of this book may be reproduced or transmitted, downloaded, distributed, reverse engineered, or stored in or introduced into any information storage and retrieval system, in any form or by any means, including photocopying and recording, whether electronic or mechanical, now known or hereinafter invented without permission in writing from the publisher.

Dorrance Publishing Co
585 Alpha Drive
Suite 103
Pittsburgh, PA 15238
Visit our website at *www.dorrancebookstore.com*

ISBN: 979-8-88925-126-2
eISBN: 979-8-88925-626-7

POEMS
of LONG AGO

Most of these poems were written in the early 40's and 50's. One of the first was *Four Seasons,* which I first titled *Roundelay.* My English professor, Miss Esther Webb liked this poem, though she called some of it trite. She encouraged me to keep writing. Some were directed toward Lila Harris, whom I was dating, and to our family after we were married. One poem was inspired by a lecturer who said there were poems about everything except a brush pile. There are poems that are whimsical, silly, and perhaps even bizarre, but I hope you will find some you will enjoy.

Dad's Story
War and Romance

My identical brother, Ray, and I, Roy, graduated from high school in Oakville, Iowa and went to work for farmers tending crops and putting up hay in the barn mow for winter feed. I had a good friend, Don Wirt in Oakville, whose mother invited me to spend the night with them whenever I was in town. I accepted a few times. One morning Don's mother said, "Roy, you have been so helpful and kind. I know you have had a rough life and lost your mother far too early. Please call me Mom." It was "Mom" from then on. Ray and I got jobs in Burlington cleaning toilets and stocking shelves. We saved enough money to buy a used car and then the stays with the Wirts became more frequent. One evening after dinner and dishes, Mom's daughter went to the piano and started playing. I stood a few feet to the side where I could watch her and enjoy her music and enjoy the presence she gave me. Mom called me aside. "You are in love with Erma, aren't you?" I don't know that I had ever heard that word before, but if that warm glow was it, then I said yes. Mom said, "she is so young, please wait." "I promise."

The United States became concerned when Japan began an aggressive military buildup and decided to build an ordinance plant in Burlington. They hired a group of young men, including Ray and I, to move materials from a rail siding to the building site. It was heavy, hard work, and by noon we were exhausted. I am not sure if we were lollygagging, but the foreman was furious. He yelled, "why don't you work like that Stoller boy? I see him twice as often as anyone else." We six brothers had a very strong bond of fellowship and camaraderie. Earl had rented a small farm with an agreement to buy it. On Thanksgiving in 1941 he asked us to come together for a meal. Earl had just purchased a savage 22 single shot rifle. He went hunting and brought back a rabbit. The brothers caught a couple pigeons. Earl dressed the rabbit and I the pigeons and slathered them with lard and baked them in the oven for our dinner. Hey, use what's available. It was a great time for us. Little did we know it would be the last time we would be together.

Then came winter and the Pearl Harbor attack. We brothers thought it appropriate to enlist. Earl was denied, saying farmers were as essential as soldiers. Arthur enlisted in the Navy and was assigned to a battleship, U.S.S. Kodoshan Bay. His battleship was hit by a kamikaze pilot. Harry enlisted in the Air Force and became a pilot. Richard enlisted in the CBs and Ray and I opted for the Air Force as fighter pilots. We were sent to Denver for exams and passed the intellectual exams and were sent for medicals. We were ordered to strip down and our manhood was checked for signs of disease. Next we were told to bend over and spread our cheeks. The medic examined me and called out for the doctor to come quick. When asked why, he replied that he had never seen a square rectum before. Now, I am not a contortionist, and it's not something I would care to see. I will just check it off as an ill sense of humor.

We were enlisted September 1942 and sent to Jefferson Barracks for our military clothes. The young lady issuing the clothes looked at Ray and then I and asked if we were both brothers, to which I replied, "no, just one of us." Taken aback for a moment, we all had a good laugh. It would be a long time before we would have another. We were sent to Florida for basic training. The upperclassmen would haze us for the next six weeks. They were not to physically touch us, but had other ways to harass us. Your manhood hangs to the left in your shorts and they required us to wear them on the right. It was very uncomfortable, but they checked us every day. For some reason they referred to them as swans. The third day I was asked if my swans were on the right side. You were not allowed to speak without permission. With it given, I said, "yes, it's on the right side, which is the left side, because it has a head of its own which is smarter than some upperclassmen." The one harassing me yelled "did you hear that?" and demanded I repeat it. They have three types of punishments, called braces. The hanging brace requires you to hang on a rafter that runs the width of the barracks to hold it together. The wall brace demands you lean against the wall at about a 90 degree angle with your neck and shoulder against the wall until you collapse. The third was a chair brace with your feet on one chair and your head on another until you could no longer hold that position and collapsed, which is the one they chose for me. But I see it as a victory, for I was never asked again, and wore my manhood where it belonged.

The harassment ended and we were sent to Sheppards Field to begin pilot training. Each student was assigned to a pilot instructor and began our daily regimen. We practiced inside and outside loops, chandelles and Immelmanns. One of our cadets died while practicing and Ray was designated to accompany the remains and the flag to his parents in Wappelo, Iowa. A week later Ray was grounded from flying. We went before the review board and reminded them that Ray had missed a week of practice by returning the body and flag to the cadet's parents. His instructor pilot refused a retest. I told them identical twins had the right to stay together and I asked to be grounded. After a short conference they ordered me to take a test flight. I did all the maneuvers carelessly, feeling I would surely be grounded. The pilot sat there for a moment and turned to me and said that was the best ride he ever had. "You are exactly the type of pilot we need." The board met again the next night and heard his report. I asked them to reinstate Ray or ground me. It would end our dream of becoming pilots, but we were determined to stay together. After some deliberation they grounded me and assigned us to a six week gunnery school to report after a three day leave.

We caught the train home and after seeing Esther, our older sister, and our brother Earl, I borrowed his car to go see the Wirts as it was getting late. Mom welcomed me and asked me to stay after they retired, because Erma wanted to talk with me. I waited in the living room until she came in and sat down beside me. Erma said, "Mom told me. Why didn't you?"

"Because I promised Mom."

"Before you leave I want you to propose to me."

"No, Erma. We don't know what the future holds, but I love you dearly, and would ask you to wait for me."

"I will."

And with that, and a long hug, I returned Earl's car and caught a train for Texas and gunnery school. Our main targets were on Padre Island, then a desolate island inhabited by rabbits and coyotes. With school completed, we were sent to Tampa Bay and assigned to a B-17 crew. We met Lt. Weaver, the pilot, and Blood, the copilot. Ray was the left waist gunner and I the tail gunner. After training together we were sent to Europe, Foggia airbase. We stopped en route at Trinidad Island and then Bellem, Brazil, before heading for Africa and Foggia, Italy. We lived in a tent with the rest of our crew. Our first bombing occurred in May of 1944. Unfortunately I cannot find the target name, though I do of others. But we came under heavy fire from flack at 30,000 feet that riddled our wings and took one engine out. Lt. Weaver feathered an engine on the other side as we headed back to base. As we approached, the third engine failed and we barely reached base. There were over a hundred holes in the wings and the plane was too heavily damaged, so they assigned us to fly Old Ironsides. On May 18, 1944, the mission to the Ploesti, Romania oil refineries took place. Our 463rd Bomb Group was sent to destroy the refinery. For that mission we received the Presidential unit citation.

On June 13, 1944 we went on a mission to the Oberpfaffenhofen Wessling air dome in Munich, Germany. On our return we were hit by flack which took out our oxygen and we had to drop down to 12,000 feet to breathe. There was solid cloud cover as we tried to return to Foggia airbase. Lt. Blood said, "don't drop any lower, there are rocks in there." Lt. Weaver spotted an opening in the clouds and dove down through it. We were in a valley surrounded by mountain peaks. A Swiss pilot appeared and waggled his wings as a signal to follow. We lit on a grassy field on the Swiss side of the Locarno river which separated the two countries. We were interrogated, stripped down, showered and fumigated, to be sure we brought nothing harmful to their country. We were quarantined for two weeks and then sent to Wengen, a small town above the Lauterbrunen valley. Our internment created an immediate concernment for Ray and I. We asked to see the managers of the hotel and said we would do the hotel laundry if we could use the facilities to do the laundry for the interned men. They agreed, and we assigned numbers for each to identify their clothes. After six months the Germans and our country agreed to a swap of detained military to be sent home. Ray and I were sent to Sioux City, Iowa and assigned desk jobs until we were discharged March 2, 1945. We had the privilege of writing our own discharge.

We enrolled in Iowa Wesleyan College for the fall term. I went to work on Earl's farm for room and board and the use of his car on Friday nights. Erma and I resumed our relationship and Mom was elated, but told me she was troubled. They had moved to Spokane, Washington, and Erma was dating a sailor. The fact that Erma never mentioned it to me was troubling. I tried to understand. She was young and lovely and needed friends, but had she broken a pledge? I vexed over this for a while and had a choice to make. Propose to her, and if she said yes, it meant getting a job and giving up my aspirations for a degree in counseling and psychology. After Ray and I returned home Esther had my box of letters and handed them back. But a choice had to be made. I went to see Erma and she was sitting on a blanket in the front yard. I approached her and dumped the box of letters at her feet. Erma looked up at me for a moment and started crying and ran into the house. That was the last time I would see her or Mom. I have never felt so hurt and sorrowful in my life, yet somehow felt I had made the right decision. I could now pursue my college goals.

Ray was married now, and we found a retired minister who had two spare bedrooms and was willing to let us stay with him in exchange for fixing meals and doing the housework. When in the Air Force, I was told by my intelligence officer that I had eidetic imagery. That meant that my mind held a picture of what I had seen or where I saw it. It was very helpful at times, but also a problem. Our economics professor made a statement that I knew was not quite accurate and I challenged him on it. I said, "if you will look on page 167, in the right quadrant, you will find your statement not substantiated." He said, "if you are so damned smart, you teach the class," and stormed out. At the next class he apologized and said it was my duty to contest a statement that was wrong. I got an A in his class, but that was not the case in physical education. I had a near drowning experience years ago and it plagued me ever since. No matter how hard I tried, I could not float or do much more than dog paddle. He knew how hard I was trying and was generous enough to give me a B. We had to teach a high school class, so when there was a future teachers convention in Davenport, Ray and I decided to attend. A group of students gathered at the wharf and Ray said, "I think I found the girl for you." He pointed to her, and I was immediately enthralled. We were getting in line to register and she was several feet ahead of me. I managed to work my way up the line by visiting with students and moving up until I was directly behind her. I was too much of an introvert to speak, but she turned and introduced herself as Lila Harris. She said she had the star role in a play, and would I care to buy a ticket? Not wanting to make her think I was just doing it to accommodate her, I bought two. I was so enchanted by my new acquaintance that I wrote an ode:

> I met a girl today. She walked
> into my life like the clean, sweet breeze
> of a balmy day of Spring. Her smile sent
> ripples dancing on the placid waters
> of Life, and they reflected the twinkling
> brightness of her eyes. She spoke - and
> the muted flute was never sweeter. The
> words cascaded like priceless pearls upon
> the soft velvet tapestry of Time. They

echoed in my heart, and struck an ancient
chord of gladness that I had never known.
I heard her name, and it lingered like the
fragrance of lavender lilacs on the country
air. "Lila," it whispered, and murmuring
softly back came - "Lila: goddess of light
and laughter, and promise of happiness
hereafter."

I did not know at the time that I had sparked an interest in me
as a possible boyfriend. Later she told me she thought I was bringing
a girlfriend to the play. When I met her at the stage door she was
pleased to see me. I asked her out for a malted milk and we had a
nice time getting acquainted. I took her home and asked if I might
see her again. She agreed and we set a date. On Sundays we usually
attended church and worked on her last college requirements. I was
finishing too. On the last class in religion Dr. Pennepacker a retired
Baptist minister was holding class. He was asking us to review what
we had learned and what questions we might have. I raised the
question of baptism and the conflicting views. I said that perhaps he
was immersed since the bible said he came up out of the water. He
exploded. "Any damned fool knows if you are in a river you have to
come up out of the water to get over the bank. Class dismissed." And
he stormed out of the classroom. I got straight As on all my tests and
all my written assignments but I got a B from him. That meant I
graduated cum laude instead of magna cum laude.

Ray and I enrolled in a masters degree program at Bradley
University in Peoria, Illinois. I arranged for a florist to deliver a
flower bowl with a rosebud to Lila and I tried to replace the bud
frequently when I returned to Burlington. My brother Richard and
his wife lived there and let me use the spare bedroom on weekends.
I would catch a bus and spend an evening with Lila before returning
to Peoria and classes. And then one day I got a letter from Lila that
tore my life apart:

May 18, 1950
Dear Roy,

Your faithful letters make me realize my own
unfaithfulness. I have been wondering for a long
time just how to write what I'm going to write and
perhaps this isn't the way, but it will be an attempt.
Roy, my friend, period. That is how I should
always like to think of you. You are not only the
most faithful, considerate, and obliging young man
I have had the pleasure to meet but more than all
these things you have been and are my most
welcome <u>friend</u>. I underlined the word to bring out
the emphasis that you are my friend and there is no
deeper feeling on my part for you to ever become
more than a friend. You, who are so forgiving,
please do not ask for my presence again. For I shall
refuse and in doing so harm our friendship. I think
you knew all along this was coming, didn't you? I
would like to express my thanks to you for the
many things you have done for me, they are greatly
appreciated and treasured, especially the poems.
We have missed you at church and our youth
groups, you do add to these things, and we are
looking forward to your return to them. I can't
explain the beauty of our yard at this time of the
year. The lovely lilacs are in full bloom and fill the
yard with their wonderful fragrance. Again and in
closing, may I thank you again for the things you
have done for me. I only hope you will be able to
find someone who will be a little more appreciative
of them than I have proved to be. In friendship
always I shall be.*

Sincerely yours,
Lila

I was in shock, for I thought we were heading for a future
together. I replied saying I will endeavor to conduct myself in
such a manner that you will not bar me from your premises, but

be able to see and yearn for the unattainable than not to see you at all.

Now I must lead you through a series of events that are almost impossible to imagine. Ray and I belong to an identical twins club. They were having a convention in St. Louis and we decided to attend. By chance we were seated by twins who lived in Peoria. During the small talk one of the twins asked what we were majoring in. When I said counseling and psychology, she said, "I wonder if you could help?" Her two year old grandson was afraid of anything furry. "Would you come over and see if you could help?" I agreed. Robbie was in a highchair and it was easy to engage him in a bit of fun. The mother and grandmother said they would go shopping and leave us alone to see what I could do. As soon as they left he was out of the highchair and onto the floor. When they returned two hours later Robbie was holding a teddy bear with his mother's fur coat across his legs. I do not know how to account for it, but it seemed to have accomplished our goal. A few days later I got a call from the grandmother saying Robbie missed me, and would I come over? It was getting late, but I agreed. Soon she said she was retiring, but I could stay with Robbie and his mother (a matchmaker in the offing?). She invited me two or three times a week to come over and I never declined if I was not busy. I never lied to her by using an excuse. Most of the time I was too involved in my assignments to accept her invitation. One evening I had a phone call from Robbie's mother. There was a movie she really wanted to see, would I take her the next evening to see the movie? I could find no legitimate excuse, so reluctantly I agreed. When we came out of the theater she met some friends and could not remember my name to introduce me. That does not do much for your ego.

In August 1950 I received a phone call from Robbie's grandmother. She said they were going to go to Burlington next Sunday, and would I meet them for lunch? Thinking quickly, I agreed on the condition that she bring Robby and his mother to meet me at the Presbyterian church that Lila and I attended. I said if she would do this, I would take them all out to lunch. She agreed and they met me at the church on Sunday. It was a small Presbyterian church that Lila and I and some friends had established in a rented building. After service, Lila came over and introduced herself to them. A few days later I received a letter from Lila's mother:

333 No. Plane St.
Burl. Ia. Tues eve.
(No! Mon. a.m. 2:30)

Dear Roy,

It's 2:30 in the morning. I can't get back to sleep. Lila & I keep talking. I told her I was coming down & get a snack & read the paper. She said "Write a letter to Roy for me," & I said O.K. She thot I meant it & she said "Oh! no! don't!" Don't you ever breath a word that I'm writing to you. Promise? Lila has grown up over nite, or shall I say over Sunday. She has taken it quite hard. You'll never know how hard it was for her to go to S.S. & Church Sunday. At first she said she wouldn't go. Do you really care for her yet or is it too late? I've always been on your side (I guess you know that). I'm thinking now of Lila's happiness. We've been talking since she came home from work. She's afraid of hurting your friend and her little boy. She cares more for you than she will let herself believe. I spoke of age diff. and she said - "Oh, not any more." Imagine she will write & tell you she wants to talk to you. May God bless you both, and help you come to the right decision.*

Love, Mrs. Harris
P.S. I'll send the poem later. I want to copy it.

I received a letter from Lila, dated August 30, 1950:

Dear Roy,

After three nights of restless sleep and tossing without coming to any decision, I decided to write to you. I'm bewildered at my own state of emotions and I need to talk with you. Roy, please come home. School begins here the fifth. Could you and would you be able to leave your studies etc. for the week end and Labor Day here? I realize it is not likely that you will be free to come after such a recent visit here but I'm hoping like everything. I feel terribly funny writing like this to you since all my indifference. My meeting with Verna and you Sunday left me in very much of a dither.*

With all hope,
Lila

I felt for her, for I had similar feelings when I received Lila's 'don't ask' letter. I returned the next Friday with some trepidation. What type of greeting would I receive? A hello, a handshake, a hug? Her "with all hope" gave me some hope too. I met her at the door. Lila greeted me with a handshake and "thank you for coming, I knew I could always trust in you, can we talk?" We spent a long time reviewing our relationship. Lila asked if we could continue and I said "yes, for I thought I had lost you forever." We ended with a date for the next night. We reviewed our first times together and growing fondness for each other. Lila said she relented her uncertainty of feelings towards me. She expressed her love for me and I said, "is there still hope for us to resume our relationship?" She said "yes, and that was my hope too. I love you more than I realized." We said our goodbyes because I had to return to Bradley for my finals.

Our relationship continued to develop and we talked of plans for the future. Her mother was pleased to see that we had resolved our differences that reinforced our love for each other. On the evening of December 10, 1950, I knelt before her and asked her if she would do me the honor of becoming my wife? I put our engagement ring on her finger and she went up to show her mother. It was her birthday. She did not come down but sent her wishes for a happy future. We announced our engagement in the Burlington Gazette. A few days later I got a phone call in the evening and when I answered all I heard was "I'll haunt you until the end of your life." Any guesses who this could be? Robbie's grandmother?

If any one of these series of events hadn't taken place, the convention in St. Louis, meeting Robbie's grandmother, curing Robbie's phobia, meeting them at the church where Lila met Verna (Robbie's mother) there would have been a different conclusion and Lila and I would never have been together again.

Lila and I made plans for the future and announced our marriage date of June 10, 1951 to start our life as husband and wife, but that is another story.

*I kept all of Lila's letters and the letter from her mother and have them in an album. The spelling is just as it was in the letters.

ROUNDELAY

Oh, the nicest time of all seems to me to be the fall,
When the harvest has begun till the harvest days are done;
When the birds begin their flight and you hear their calls at night
When the leaves commence to fall and the squirrels start to call;
When the white clouds scurry by past the moon that sails on high;
And you see their shadows flee 'cross the grass and 'cross the sea.
Yes, the nicest time of all seems to me to be the fall --

Till I remember days of spring when the birds begin to sing.
Then the nicest time is had in the spring that makes us glad.
When days are getting longer and the sun is shining stronger;
When the seeds begin to sprout and the insect world comes out.
When the wind is sailing kites and the rains come down at nights.
When the world seems fresh and new and the sky seems brighter, too.
Yes, the spring to me seems best till I think of all the rest --

That the summer brings to me in the days that are so free.
Now the days are extra long, filled with laughter, gay with song.
There is time to play and run or to lie out in the sun.
There's a swimming hole or pool when days are hot and water cool.
There is fishing in the lake and a picnic lunch to take.
There are lots of things to do and life's problems then are few
When the summer time is here and the world is full of cheer.

Yet the winter time seems best when you think of all the rest,
For the joys it has in store are a hundred-fold or more.
The world becomes a wonderland of frost and ice, snow so grand;
Some times the drifts pile high and snowball battles fill the sky.
Sleds come sailing down the hill and some tip over for a spill.
Forts and snowmen we can make till the toes and fingers ache.
Yes, winter seems best of all till I think again of fall.

Four Seasons (first titled as Roundelay)

Oh, the nicest time of all seems to me to be the fall,
When the harvest has begun till the harvest days are done;
When the birds begin their flight and you hear their calls at night;
When the leaves commence to fall and the squirrels start to call;
When the white clouds scurry by past the moon that sails on high;
And you see their shadows flee 'cross the grass and 'cross the sea.
Yes, the nicest time of all seems to me to be the fall - -

Till I remember days of spring when the birds begin to sing.
Then the nicest time is had in the spring that makes us glad.
When days are getting longer and the sun is shining stronger;
When the seeds begin to sprout and the insect world comes out.
When the wind is sailing kites and the rains come down at nights.
When the world seems fresh and new and the sky seems brighter, too.
Yes, the spring to me seems best till I think of all the rest - -

That the summer brings to me in the days that are so free.
Now the days are extra long, filled with laughter, gay with song.
There is time to play and run or to lie out in the sun.
There's a swimming hole or pool when days are hot and water cool.
There is fishing in the lake and a picnic lunch to take.
There are lots of things to do and life's problems then are few.
When the summer time is here and the world is full of cheer.

Yet the winter time seems best when you think of all the rest,
For the joys it has in store are a hundred-fold or more.
The world becomes a wonderland of frost and ice, snow so grand;
Some times the drifts pile high and snowball battles fill the sky.
Sleds come sailing down the hill and some tip over for a spill.
Forts and snowmen we can make till the toes and fingers ache.
Yes, winter seems best of all till I think again of fall.

Roy H. Stoller

Ode to a Brushpile

O Twisted limbs and broken bough,
And twigs that once were tree:
As you lie dead and useless now
So I shall someday be.
But you once a shelter made
With heavenward head and feet on ground.
Safe in your arms God's creatures stayed,
And food there and rest they found.
You inspired the poet to praise
And with your greatness born of sod
Have humbled heart and caused to raise
Man's voice in reverence to God.
My prayer now would humbly be
That I may yet, 'ere I am dead,
Inspire and teach as you -- a tree --
And Man's sould to Got hath lead.

Ode to a Brushpile

O twisted limbs and broken bough,
And twigs that once were tree:
As you lie dead and useless now
So I shall someday be.
But you once a shelter made
With heavenward head and feet on ground.
Safe in your arms God's creatures stayed,
And food there and rest they found.
You inspired the poet to praise
And with your greatness born of sod
Have humbled heart and caused to raise
Man's voice in reverence to God.
My prayer now would humbly be
That I may yet, 'ere I am dead,
Inspire and teach as you - - a tree - -
And Man's soul to God hath lead.

Dad's note:

Dad and Mom attended a conference. The speaker
noted that there were poems to everything except
a brushpile. Dad's reply was this poem.

                              A Rose

The melting snow, the thawing earth
Awoke the world to Nature's birth;
A tiny seed, a shower, a little soil,
And rays of the sun began to toil.
The showers, soil, Spring's bright sun--
And Nature's work was just begun:
The seed put forth a probing root,
Followed this with a thriving shoot;
One reached down and the other up,
Using God's earth for a drinking cup.

The roots sank deeper while they dined,
The shoot to heaven its arms entwined.
The fruit brought forth for us to see
Will warm our hearts until eternity;
Perfect art when its leaves are curled,
It is matchless beauty when unfurled.
One new little bud, though all alone,
Cannot be by a star outshone.
Corsage, bouquet, in other ways,
They add loveliness to our days.

Each flower, until its life is spent,
Brings priceless beauty to the firmament.
Its own perfection and fragrant smell
Speak its beauty more than voice can tell.
When words fail as they sometimes do,
They'll speak out your thoughts for you.
Whether it's sympathy in sorrow,
Special occasions, a promise for tomorrow,
The perfect courier--everyone knows--
Is nothing more than just a rose.

                                  by Roy H. Stoller

A Rose

The melting snow, the thawing earth
Awoke the world to Nature's birth;
A tiny seed, a shower, a little soil,
And rays of the sun began to toil.
The showers, soil, Spring's bright sun - -
And Nature's work was just begun:
The seed put forth a probing root,
Followed this with a thriving shoot;
One reached down and the other up,
Using God's earth for a drinking cup.

The roots sank deeper while they dined,
The shoot to heaven its arms entwined.
The fruit brought forth for us to see
Will warm our hearts until eternity;
Perfect art when its leaves are curled,
It is matchless beauty when unfurled.
One new little bud, though all alone,
Cannot be by a star outshone.
Corsage, bouquet, in other ways,
They add loveliness to our days.

Each flower, until its life is spent,
Brings priceless beauty to the firmament.
Its own perfection and fragrant smell
Speak its beauty more than voice can tell.
When words fail as they sometimes do,
They'll speak out your thoughts for you.
Whether it's sympathy in sorrow,
Special occasions, a promise for tomorrow,
The perfect courier - - everyone knows - -
Is nothing more than just a rose.

Roy H. Stoller

A Little Boy's Thoughts

When I lie down to take my nap,
Then I put on my "thinking cap".

I think of what I'd like to be:
Perhaps a sailor on the sea,

And visit lands that are strange;
Or be a cowboy on the range,

And ride my horse across the plains.
A doctor stops your aches and pains

And that would be so nice to do,
Or I could play sweet songs for you

If I would learn to lead a band.
A farmer has lots of land

And grows fine crops that we can eat.
To fly a plane is hard to beat

For that sounds like a lot of fun.
But then when all is said and done,

Regardless of the thoughts I've had,
I'd rather be just like my Dad!

A Little Boy's Thoughts

When I lie down to take my nap
Then I put on my "thinking cap".

I think of what I'd like to be;
Perhaps a sailor on the sea,

And visit lands that are so strange;
Or be a cowboy on the range,

And ride my horse across the plains.
A doctor stops your aches and pains

And that would be so nice to do.
Or I could play sweet songs for you

If I would learn to lead a band.
A farmer has a lot of land

And grows fine crops that we can eat.
To fly a plane is hard to beat,

For that sounds like a lot of fun.
But then when all is said and done,

Regardless of the thoughts I've had,
I'd rather be just like my Dad!

I met a girl today. She walked into my life
like the clean, sweet breeze of a balmy day of spring.
Her smile sent ripples dancing on the placid waters of
Life, and they reflected the twinkling brightness of
her eyes. She spoke - and the muted flute was never
sweeter. The words cascaded like priceless pearls
upon the soft velvet tapestry of Time. They echoed
in my heart, and struck an ancient chord of gladness
that I had never known. I heard her name, and it
lingered like the fragrance of lavender lilacs on the
country air. "Lila", it whispered, and murmuring
softly back came - "Lila: goddess of light and
laughter, and promise of happiness hereafter."

I met a girl today. She walked
into my life like the clean, sweet breeze
of a balmy day of spring. Her smile sent
ripples dancing on the placid waters
of Life, and they reflected the twinkling
brightness of her eyes. She spoke - and
the muted flute was never sweeter. The
words cascaded like priceless pearls upon
the soft velvet tapestry of Time. They
echoed in my heart, and struck an ancient
chord of gladness that I had never known.
I heard her name, and it lingered like the
fragrance of lavender lilacs on the country
air. "Lila," it whispered, and murmuring
softly back came - "Lila: goddess of light
and laughter, and promise of happiness
hereafter."

Dad's Poem to Mom

I met a girl today. She walked
into my life like the clean, sweet breeze
of a balmy day of Spring. Her smile sent
ripples dancing on the placid waters
of Life, and they reflected the twinkling
brightness of her eyes. She spoke - and
the muted flute was never sweeter. The
words cascaded like priceless pearls upon
the soft velvet tapestry of Time. They
echoed in my heart, and struck an ancient
chord of gladness that I had never known.
I heard her name, and it lingered like the
fragrance of lavender lilacs on the country
air. "Lila", it whispered, and murmuring
softly back came – "Lila: goddess of light
and laughter, and promise of happiness
hereafter."

Dad's note:

We met at a future teacher's convention in
Davenport, Iowa. Lila was standing in front of me
in line to register and introduced herself. She was
to be in a play and asked if I wanted to buy a ticket
(I bought two). After the play, I met her at the stage
door and invited her out for refreshments and took
her home. This was the beginning of our
relationship.

"If I had my life to live over",
I've heard some folks say,
"I'd sure reconsider and do
Things in a different way."

Now, what kind of living, I ask,
Could they have faced
To make them wish it were changed
Or have it replaced?

Are they not happy?, I wonder,
With their choice of friends?
Have they no loved ones to seek
When their day's work ends?

Have their mistakes not helped them,
Through experience, to learn?
Is "what I give" not as vital
As merely "What I earn"?

If a chance to live my life over
Were to give me a call,
I'd do the things I have done
-- But sooner, that's all!

If I Had My Life to Live Over

"If I had my life to live over",
I've heard some folks say,
"I'd sure reconsider and do
Things in a different way."

Now, what kind of living, I ask,
Could they have faced
To make them wish it were changed
Or have it replaced?

Are they not happy?, I wonder,
With their choice of friends?
Have they no loved ones to seek
When their day's work ends?

Have their mistakes not helped them,
Through experience, to learn?
Is "what I give" not as vital
As merely "What I earn"?

If a chance to live my life over
Were to give me a call,
I'd do the things I have done
- - But sooner, that's all!

In Captivity

You've captured my thoughts-- as you often do;
My heart cries out as it longs for you.
You're on my mind as you often are.
Whether you're near or when afar.
But the thoughts of you -- as they come to me
In the quiet hours of my reverie --
Are a mixture of joys mingled with tears;
A hundred hopes seamed with fears.
For my love for you, as it continues to grow,
Is turned aside with a forceful. "No."
You say your love for me can never be,
But mine will last to eternity.
Though you spurn me --love deny,
I'll love you till the day I die.

Roy W. Stoller

In Captivity

You've captured my thoughts - - as you often do;
My heart cries out as it longs for you.
You're on my mind as you often are,
Whether you're near or when afar.
But the thoughts of you - - as they come to me
In the quiet hours of my reverie - -
Are a mixture of joys mingled with tears;
A hundred hopes seamed with fears.
For my love for you, as it continues to grow,
Is turned aside with a forceful, "No."
You say your love for me can never be,
But mine will last to eternity.
Though you spurn me - - love deny,
I'll love you till the day I die.

Just a Rose

Just a rose that buds and blooms--
and then is gone;
Just a rose, but its memory
lingers on.
For while it lived, and was
with us yet,
It plighted a troth we could
not forget;
It promised to us that while
it should live,
All of its beauty it would
fragrantly give.
And as it blossomed so
wondrous, fair,
It perfumed the room and
sweetened the air.
It so gladly lived, and
it freely died,
That our fleeting joys might
be multiplied.
Here's to the rose we so
joyously hail,
Though its petals may wither
and perfume fail:
Just a rose that buds and blooms--
and then is gone;
Just a rose, but its memory
lingers on.

Just a Rose

Just a rose that buds and blooms - -
and then is gone;
Just a rose, but its memory
lingers on.
For while it lived, and was
with us yet,
It plighted a troth we could
not forget;
It promised to us that while
it should live,
All of its beauty it would
fragrantly give.
And as it blossomed so
wondrous, fair,
It perfumed the room and
sweetened the air.
It so gladly lived, and
it freely died,
That our fleeting joys might
be multiplied.
Here's to the rose we so
joyously hail,
Though its petals may wither
and perfume fail:
Just a rose that buds and blooms - -
and then is gone;
Just a rose, but its memory
lingers on.

Just as Brave

I think about the days of old
And wonder if they were so bold --
The boys and girls who lived in them --
As my folks know that now I am.
Oh, they had dragons to beware.
And there were other dangers there,
Like tigers, lions, and other beasts.
And famines often followed feasts.
Pestilence and fire took their lot,
But these are enemies we've still got.
If they had times of tear and woe,
So be it now; 'tis ever so.
In place of dragons now to dread
We have the atom bomb instead.
That threat is much more real, I'm sure
than fiery beasts they could conjure.
Instead of tigers, we have cars
To kill and maim and leave their scars.
Why just to cross our city streets
Matches the danger of their feats.
They may have had a lot to fear;
We face as much most every year.
When you consider what we face --
The dangers of the human race --
We're just as brave and just as bold
As boys and girls in days of old.

Just as Brave

I think about the days of old
And wonder if they were so bold - -
The boys and girls who lived in them - -
As my folks know that now I am.
Oh, they had dragons to beware.
And there were other dangers there,
Like tigers, lions, and other beasts.
And famines often followed feasts.
Pestilence and fire took their lot,
But these are enemies we've still got.
If they had times of tear and woe,
So be it now; 'tis ever so.
In place of dragons now to dread
We have the atom bomb instead.
That threat is much more real, I'm sure
than fiery beasts they could conjure.
Instead of tigers, we have cars
To kill and maim and leave their scars.
Why just to cross our city streets
Matches the danger of their feats.
They may have had a lot to fear;
We face as much most every year.
When you consider what we face - -
The dangers of the human race - -
We're just as brave and just as bold
As boys and girls in days of old.

                    Light of my Life

Light of my life, my love, my laughter,
Promise of hope and happiness hereafter:
Each tiring day departs and leaves behind
Some cherished memory of you within my mind.
Each new day brings something new
And adds it to my thoughts of you;
Some word you spoke, a smile for me --
Each finds a place in my reverie.

My life holds hope that you will give
Your heart to me that I may live.
And I, in turn, will pledge to you
A heart that is loyal, kind, and true.
You are my love, light of my life;
I'm asking you, Darling: "Be my wife."

                                        Roger Steele

Light of My Life

Light of my life, my love, my laughter,
Promise of hope and happiness hereafter:
Each tiring day departs and leaves behind
Some cherished memory of you within my mind.
Each new day brings something new
And adds it to my thoughts of you;
Some word you spoke, a smile for me - -
Each finds a place in my reverie.
My life holds hope that you will give
Your heart to me that I may live.
And I, in turn, will pledge to you
A heart that is loyal, kind, and true.
You are my love, light of my life;
I'm asking you, Darling: "Be my wife."

Love

We meet, and fall in love, and part;
But still we do not die of a broken heart.
We wish we could, it pains us so:
Oh, God! Relieve us of that bitter throe!

Time, and time alone, will dull the pain,
While we sit and weep and cry in vain.
But when our hearts are not so sore,
Why must it happen to us once more?

Oh, why is it we must live, and grieve,
And let false love so oft' deceive?
Is there no way that we can efface
This pitfall of the human race?

Lord, destroy this sorrow, grief, and woe;
And in its place let true love grow.
Let grow the love like that of ours,
That knows no minutes, days, or hours.

And when the death bell tolls its knell,
Lead us far away from hell.
Give us a home up there above,
And with us share your generous love.

Love

We meet, and fall in love, and part;
But still we do not die of a broken heart.
We wish we could, it pains us so:
Oh, God! Relieve us of that bitter throe!

Time, and time alone, will dull the pain,
While we sit and weep and cry in vain.
But when our hearts are not so sore,
Why must it happen to us once more?

Oh, why is it we must live, and grieve,
And let false love so oft' deceive?
Is there no way that we can efface
This pitfall of the human race?

Lord, destroy this sorrow, grief, and woe;
And in its place let true love grow.
Let grow the love like that of ours,
That knows no minutes, days, or hours.

And when the death bell tolls its knell,
Lead us far away from Hell.
Give us a home up there above,
And with us share your generous love.

My Dilemma

I'm a twin and I've got my trouble.
And for brother, hay, that goes double.

We've tried wearing different style clothes
But which one is me still nobody knows.

I've tried growing a mustache on my lip;
Long hair, short hair, and a Kelly Clip.

Horn-rimmed glasses and painted nails,
And everything else just simply fails.

We used to think it was rather amusing;
but now hay's married, and it's confusing.

For all the single girls look rather married,
Wondering which is single and which is married.

Now I'd like to have one date
before I get to be eighty-eight.

So here is my one and only plea:
how can they tell which one is me?

My Dilemma

I'm a twin and I've got my trouble.
And for brother, Ray, that goes double.

We've tried wearing different style clothes
But which one is me still nobody knows.

I've tried growing a mustache on my lip;
Long hair, short hair, and a Kelly clip.

Horn-rimmed glasses and painted nails,
And everything else just simply fails.

We used to think it was rather amusing;
But now Ray's married, and it's confusing.

For all the single girls look rather harried,
Wondering which is single and which is married.

Now I'd like to have one date
Before I get to be eighty-eight.

So here is my one and only plea:
How can they tell which one is me?

My Mother-in-law

I've hear it said (and so have you!)
That Mother-in-laws should be taboo,
And some folks seem to have a fear
Most every time that she comes near.
There are those who speak to their's
In a gruff voice resembling a bear's.
And some are rude as they can be
And "wonder why she's not nice to me?"
Now it may be there are a few
That some have cause to really rue,
But when I speak of Mother-in-laws
I never hesitate, or even pause,
To say that there is none so fine
As this dear mother-in-law of mine.

My Mother-in-law

I've heard it said (and so have you!)
That Mother-in-laws should be taboo,
And some folks seem to have a fear
Most every time that she comes near.
There are those who speak to their's
In a gruff voice resembling a bear's.
And some are rude as they can be
And "wonder why she's not nice to me?"
Now it may be there are a few
That some have cause to really rue,
But when I speak of Mother-in-laws
I never hesitate, or even pause,
To say that there is none so fine
As this dear mother-in-law of mine.

Dad's Note:

This was brought to mind when a group of men
raised the subject. One blamed his mother-in-law
for his divorce from his wife. Another said his was
a constant source of trouble in the home. And a
third said his was often the cause of friction in the
family. Of the four in the room, I apparently, was
the only one who could speak with praise of my
relationship with my mother-in-law.

Nails

Here are Daddy's nails so very nice and straight.
Here is Daddy's hammer; it's a lot of weight.
I tried to pound the nails and down the hammer went.
Oh! see what happened? Daddy's nails are bent.

Nails

Here are Daddy's nails so very nice and straight.
Here is Daddy's hammer; it's a lot of weight.
I tried to pound the nails and down the hammer went.
Oh! see what happened? Daddy's nails are bent.

Pushing Pete

Once there lived a little boy who was always pushing his little
playmates. When they weren't looking he would push them, and he
would shove them when they were. To him it didn't matter if they
were playing ball: he didn't seem to care if they might fall;
He pushed them on the sidewalk and he pushed them on the dirt.
He laughed to seem them cry, and smiled when they were hurt.
He pushed when others joined in play. He pushed them almost every day.
Now, for his friends this was not fun, and so they left him, one by one.
They would not play with him at all, for fear they might be pushed and fall.
So Pusher Pete was left alone with not a friend to call his own.
No one called for him to round and join in any game of fun.
Alone he stood and -- Now quite said: he'd pushed away all friends he had.
It"It must be nice," he thought, aloud -- "to join in sucha happy crowd
of boys and girls who laugh and play. Andhave such fun with friends
each day.
If only I had three wishes now, I'd spend them wisely; this is how:
I'd wish that I had never pushed, and then
I'd wish each one was my friend again,
And then I'd wish for them to say:
Oh, please, Pete, come on and play."

Roy H. Stolts

Pushing Pete

Once there lived a little boy who was always pushing his little playmates. When they weren't looking he would push them, and he would shove them when they were. To him it didn't matter if they were playing ball; He didn't seem to care if they might fall;
He pushed them on the sidewalk and he pushed them on the dirt.
He laughed to see them cry, and smiled when they were hurt.
He pushed when others joined in play. He pushed them almost every day.
Now, for his friends this was not fun, and so they left him, one by one.
They would not play with him at all, for fear they might be pushed and fall.
So Pusher Pete was left alone with not a friend to call his own.
No one called for him to run and join in any game of fun.
Alone he stood and - - Now quite sad; He'd pushed away all friends he had.
"It must be nice," he thought, aloud - - "to join in such a happy crowd of boys and girls who laugh and play. And have such fun with friends each day.
If only I had three wishes now, I'd spend them wisely; this is how:
I'd wish that I had never pushed, and then
I'd wish each one was my friend again,
And then I'd wish for them to say:
Oh, please, Pete, come on and play."

St. Valentine's Day

The fourteenth day of February: St. Valentine's
Day
Is set aside to show your love in a pleasant
way.
Be it a song or a gift, a card or a letter,
It's all to express your love the better.
So as sure as the angels watch from above,
I'm sure you know it is you that I love.
But under only one condition I'll give you
my heart:
You must handle it gently until death bids
us part.
If you'll agree to this last line,
Then I'll have you for my Valentine.

                              By
                              Roy H. Stoller

St. Valentine's Day

The fourteenth day of February: St. Valentine's Day
Is set aside to show your love in a pleasant way.
Be it a song or a gift, a card or a letter,
It's all to express your love the better.
So as sure as the angels watch from above,
I'm sure you know it is you that I love.
But under only one condition I'll give you my heart:
You must handle it gently until death bids us part.
If you'll agree to this last line,
Then I'll have you for my Valentine.

Take My Love

I want so much to be with you
And share in all the things you do;
I want your every act to be
Part of my life, my heart, and me.

Let me share your joy and gladness;
Let me bear your grief and sadness.
Give me your smiles and shed no tears;
Take my love and have no fears.

In the twilight of our life,
I the husband, you the wife,
We'll relive the days gone by
Of life full-lived: you and I.

We'll recall the storm and strife,
But most of all, a happy life;
When mortal life for us is ending,
Two hears as one yet ever blending.

But come, my dear, let's not delay;
Life is hurrying on its way.
It's a one-way-trip, you know;
Come, let's share it as we go!

Roy H. Stoller

Take My Love (first titled as Sharing)

I want so much to be with you
And share in all the things you do;
I want your every act to be
Part of my life, my heart, and me.

Let me share your joy and gladness;
Let me bear your grief and sadness.
Give me your smiles and shed no tears;
Take my love and have no fears.

In the twilight of our life,
I the husband, you the wife,
We'll relive the days gone by
Of life full-lived - - you and I.

We'll recall the storm and strife,
But most of all, a happy life;
When mortal life for us is ending,
Two hearts as one yet ever blending.

But come, my Dear, let's not delay;
Life is hurrying on its way.
It's a one-way-trip, you know;
Come, let's share it as we go!

The Awakening

Away down deep in ol' Mother Earth
Lay a little tiny seed just a 'waitin' birth.
Said he to himself, "Now why don't I
Push up to the sun; I can if I try."
So he struggled out of his little pod
And put out a leaf (with the help of God).
The leaf opened up and began to toil,
And so did the roots deep down in the soil.
And before very long it was plain to see
That seed was strivin' to become a tree:

Though we're quite little, in deeds very small,
We can prove our worth, and in Faith be tall.
And in Truth -- though we only start from "scratch"--
We can find our Trust and our Strength to match.

The Awakening

Away down deep in ol' Mother Earth
Lay a little tiny seed just a 'waitin' birth.
Said he to himself, "Now why don't I
Push up to the sun; I can if I try."
So he struggled out of his little pod
and put out a leaf (with the help of God).
The leaf opened up and began to toil,
And so did the roots deep down in the soil.
And before very long it was plain to see
That seed was strivin' to become a tree:

Though we're quite little, in deeds very small,
We can prove our worth, and in Faith be tall.
And in Truth - - though we only start from "scratch" - -
We can find our Trust and our Strength to match.

The Magic Land of Dreams

It's a magic land to where we go,
This strange place of many sleeps;
And I doubt if we will ever know
All the mysteries it keeps.

But it is fun to close our eyes
And explore them one by one;
Anf if a person really tries
His journey is soon begun.

Sailing away on a great white cloud
To explore the world so wide,
I can be a king so fine and proud
With a big white horse to ride.

I can be a giant in the sky
With strength of iron in my arm,
But so softly step that a fly
Would never come to any harm.

I can be as small as any elf
That walks the garden green,
And hide my tiny fairy self
Where I am never seen.

I am an airplane or a train,
If that is my desire.
I am the rainbow in the rain,
A fire truck at a fire.

I can be an important mayor,
If my fancy chooses;
Or be the best baseball player:
(One that never loses).

And no matter how far I go
Or what adventures take,
It is always nice to know
I am back when I awake.

Roy A. Stoller

The Magic Land of Dreams

It's a magic land to where we go,
This strange place of many sleeps;
And I doubt if we will ever know
All the mysteries it keeps.

But it is fun to close our eyes
And explore them one by one;
And if a person really tries
His journey is soon begun.

Sailing away on a great white cloud
To explore the world so wide,
I can be a king so fine and proud
With a big white horse to ride.

I can be a giant in the sky
With strength of iron in my arm,
But so softly step that a fly
Would never come to any harm.

I can be as small as any elf
That walks the garden green,
And hide my tiny fairy self
Where I am never seen.

I am an airplane or a train,
If that is my desire.
I am the rainbow in the rain,
A fire truck at a fire.

I can be an important mayor,
If my fancy chooses,
Or be the best baseball player
(One that never loses).

And no matter how far I go
Or what adventures take,
It is always nice to know
I am back when I awake.

PRISCILLA

A rose for one who knows
The secret of my heart;
May the beauty as it grows,
When the perfumed petals part,
Let the pure love that flows
Find in you a yielding heart.

Let its presence in your room--
And the beauty that you see--
Dispense with any trace of gloom,
Invoke the day that soon will be
When your love begins to bloom,
And that love is just for me.

The Presence

A rose for one who knows
The secret of my heart;
May the beauty as it grows,
When the perfumed petals part,
Let the pure love that flows
Find in you a yielding heart.

Let its presence in your room - -
And the beauty that you see - -
Dispense with any trace of gloom,
Invoke the day that soon will be
When your love begins to bloom,
And that love is just for me.

The Stars at Play

In the sky at night
If you look just right,
You will see a sight
As the stars so bright
Begin to play.

Though the night is long
They will burst into song
As they gather and throng
And as they dance along
The Milky Way.

See them twinkle and shine
As they form a chorus line,
When the weather is fine,
And their world is mine
'Till another day.

See them all come out
As they seem to shout
That the night, no doubt,
Was made to dance about
While feeling gay.

Are they calling my name,
As they flicker and flame,
To join in their game
And pretend I'm the same
'Till it is day?

Were I a bright star
Out there, Oh, so far
Where all others stars are,
No child would I bar
To come and play.

Roy H. Stoller

The Stars at Play

In the sky at night,
If you look just right,
You will see a sight
As the stars so bright
Begin to play.

Though the night is long
They will burst into song
As they gather and throng
And as the dance along
The Milky Way.

See them twinkle and shine
As they form a chorus line,
When the weather is fine
And their world is mine
'Till another day.

See them all come out
As they seem to shout
That the night, no doubt,
Was made to dance about
While feeling gay.

Are they calling my name,
As they flicker and flame,
To join in their game
And pretend I'm the same
'Till it is day?

Were I a bright star
Out there, Oh, so far
Where all other stars are,
No child would I bar
To come and play.

Treasured Time

How long, my love, since we've been wed?
Days and months into years have sped.
But who counts time by days or nights?
Three thousand kisses that I treasure
Are to me a better measure
Of the time we've shared delights
Of married life and wedded bliss,
Since lips first met in nuptial kiss.
Caressing hands and gentle touch,
Ten thousand smiles, that convey
What words sometimes can never say,
Through the years have meant so much.
And moments, too, of quietness
Whisper "love" in soft caress.
I think we will both agree,
The years that we've been man and wife
Are few compared to those in life.
But they've been best, by far, for me.

Treasured Time

How long, my love, since we've been wed?
Days and months into years have sped.
But who counts time by days or nights?
Three thousand kisses that I treasure
Are to me a better measure
Of the time we've shared delights
Of married life and wedded bliss,
Since lips first met in nuptial kiss.
Caressing hands and gentle touch,
Ten thousand smiles, that convey
What words sometimes can never say,
Through the years have meant so much.
And moments, too, of quietness
Whisper "love" in soft caress.
I think we will both agree,
The years that we've been man and wife
Are few compared to those in life.
But they've been best, by far, for me.

'Till Break of Day

In the quiet comfort of a summer night,
The silent wings of love take flight.
And lead my eager heart astray.
There, embraced by love's enchanting heights,
my lips, my arms, seek new delights --
And you are mine till break of day.

'Till Break of Day

In the quiet comfort of a summer night,
The silent wings of love take flight.
And lead my eager heart astray.
There, embraced by love's enchanting heights,
My lips, my arms, seek new delights - -
And you are mine till break of day.

Who Needs to Dream?

There is not, in this world of ours,
A million dreams, though they were mine
But for the dreaming,
That would make me love you less;
Nor is there, on this earth of ours,
A million schemes, though they were mine
But for the scheming,
That could take your tenderness,
And leave me with more than I have now.
For no dream or no scheme of mere man upon this sod
Could e'er compare with the handiwork of God.
From whatever source He drew
The miracle that is you,
Man could not gain the wherefor or the how.
And greater miracle than this I could not pursue
In all my dreams: the day He brought me you.

Who Needs to Dream?

There is not, in this world of ours,
A million dreams, though they were mine
But for the dreaming,
That would make me love you less;
Nor is there, on this earth of ours,
A million schemes, though they were mine
But for the scheming,
That could take your tenderness,
And leave me with more than I have now.
For no dream or no scheme of mere man upon this sod
Could e'er compare with the handiwork of God.
From whatever source He drew
The miracle that is you,
Man could not gain the wherefor or the how.
And greater miracle than this I could not pursue
In all my dreams: the day He brought me you.

ANIMAL POEMS

Strange Behavior

In a trunk
In a hole,
Lived a skunk,
Lived a mole.

In the night,
In the day,
They would fight,
They would play.

They were friend,
They were foe,
Till the end
It was so.

They had fun.
They had work;
They had none
They did shirk.

From their home
In the dark
They would roam
For a lark.

Then one night
(Day was done),
Came a light
And a gun.

Men and hound
Came in sight.
Mournful sound,
Dreadful fight.

Man had fled
Scent with fright,
Dog was dead.
(Moles can bite.).

Strange Behavior

In a trunk
In a hole,
Lived a skunk,
Lived a mole.

In the night,
In the day,
They would fight,
They would play.

They were friend,
They were foe,
Till the end
It was so.

They had fun,
They had work;
They had none
They did shirk.

From their home
In the dark
They would roam
For a lark.

Then one night
(Day was done),
Came a light
And a gun.

Man and hound
Came in sight.
Mournful sound,
Dreadful fight.

Man had fled
Scent with fright,
Dog was dead.
(Moles can bite.).

Two little love birds out on a limb:
One named Pat and the other one Tim.

Pat preened and primped in the summer air,
While Tim sang loudly for his lady fair.

They basked in the sun, while in the sky
The fleecy clouds and their dreams sailed by.

For they were young and this was fun
To cuddle and coo in the summer sun.

My Love's not Pat and I'm not Tim
We'd never trade with her and him.

For they don't have a hundred ways
To speak their love and sing their praise.

To confide, comfort, and caress
Or show their love their happiness.

Two Little Love Birds

Two little love birds out on a limb;
One named Pat and the other one Tim.

Pat preened and primped in the summer air,
While Tim sang loudly for his lady fair.

They basked in the sun, while in the sky
The fleecy clouds and their dreams sailed by.

For they were young and this was fun
To cuddle and coo in the summer sun.

My Love's not Pat and I'm not Tim
We'd never trade with her and him.

For they don't have a hundred ways
To speak their love and sing their praise.

To confide, comfort, and caress
Or show their love their happiness.

Spinning Spider

Watch the little spider climbing on his thread.
See the little spider spinning on his web.
Now he brings it down, then
Up he goes again,
Until he's gone around with another silken thread.
That's how the spider spins his pretty web.

Spinning Spider

Watch the little spider climbing on his thread.
See the little spider spinning on his web.
Now he brings it down, then
Up he goes again,
Until he's gone around with another silken thread.
That's how the spider spins his pretty web.

Consider the Cat

The cat is an animal of much regard. Empresses of old had them to pet,
And if you look in palaces you'll find them there yet.
But a child that's as poor as the poorest mouse
Can have a cat, too, to reside in his house.
Pedigreed of any breed, it matters not how big and fat,
Are loved no more than some poor urchin's alley cat.
Cats stay up and go out late most every night,
And sleep when they're tired, which seems to be right.
They wash their face and clean their paws, though after they have
had their meal.
They yawn or stretch, or purr contentment, and show the moods
they feel.
Cats won't go in where the whiskers on their cheeks won't go --
"Using their heads - That's what they're for", someone told me so.
And though its eyes are open and its ears are keen,
It doesn't repeat what it has heard or what it has seen.
A cat takes what life offers as it comes its way
And finds time to be happy a little each day.
No ulcers to show for worry and strife,
It makes the most of every-day life.
Now there's a lesson to learn form thecat:
Why can't you and I be more like that?

Consider the Cat

The cat is an animal of much regard. Empresses of old had them to pet.
And if you look in the palaces you'll find them there yet.
But a child that's as poor as the poorest mouse
Can have a cat, too, to reside in his house.
Pedigreed of any breed, it matters not how big and fat,
Are loved no more than some poor urchin's alley cat.
Cats stay up and go out late most every night,
And sleep when they're tired, which seems to be right.
They wash their face and clean their paws, though after they have
had their meal.
They yawn or stretch, or purr contentment, and show the moods
they feel.
Cats won't go in where the whiskers on their cheeks won't go - -
"Using their heads – That's what they're for", someone told me so.
And though its eyes are open and its ears are keen,
It doesn't repeat what it has heard or what it has seen.
A cat takes what life offers as it comes its way
And finds time to be happy a little each day.
No ulcers to show for worry and strife,
It makes the most of every-day life.
Now there's a lesson to learn from the cat:
Why can't you and I be more like that?

Mr. Rabbit and Mr. Rat

Mister Rabbit and Mister Rat
Went to sea in a big brown hat.
The hat sank in up to the brim;
Said Mr. Rabbit, "I can't swim!"
"Mister Rabbit", said Mister Rat,
"Now you just hold on to your hat.
Lean out your side and with your hand
Paddle water to beat the band."
They paddled to and paddled fro
Just as fast as their hands could go.
Both paddled hard with all their might
But still no land came into sight.
(If you haven't guessed if before,
Each was trying for another shore).
Their hands grew tired, their arms did too,
Until they didn't know what to do.
So one used his tail, one his ears,
And they paddled this way for years.
That's why the rat's tail's so strong
And why the rabbit's ears are long.

Mr. Rabbit and Mr. Rat

Mr. Rabbit and Mister Rat
Went to sea in a big brown hat.
The hat sank in up to the brim;
Said Mr. Rabbit, "I can't swim!"
"Mister Rabbit", said Mister Rat,
"Now you just hold on to your hat.
Lean out your side and with your hand
Paddle water to beat the band."
They paddled to and paddled fro
Just as fast as their paws could go.
Both paddled hard with all their might
But still no land came into sight.
(If you haven't guessed it before,
Each was trying for the other shore.)
Their paws grew tired, legs did too,
Until they didn't know what to do.
So one used his tail, one his ears,
And they paddled this way for years.
That's why the rat's tail is so strong
And why the rabbit's ears are long.

The Considerate Cat

A country cat came in to town
To see his city cousin.
That is, to see the one named Brown.
(He had at least a dozen).

Now cousin Brown was very rich,
Oh, very rich indeed,
For he controlled a fortune which
Was made in catnip seed.

He had a big apartment house,
A fancy car to drive,
And he ate only "imported mouse"
(And on them he did thrive).

For he was fat as any cat
Which I have ever seen.
And though it's true that he was fat,
He also kept quite clean.

He washed his face before each meal
And washed when he was through.
He knew how good it made him feel
(And surely you do too!)

The country cat was much impressed
With all that he had seen.
His cousin Brown was neatly dressed.
(If you know what I mean.).

He always kept his clothes so neat
They almost looked like new,
Clear from his hat down to his feet.
(Perhaps that's just like you).

And city cat said "Thank you, Sir",
And "Please" and also "Pardon".
For, just as if his manners were
A pretty flower garden,

He gave them tender care each day.
And I'm sure you will find,
If you're just as nice, folks will say
That you're the thoughtful kind.

The country cat enjoyed his stay
With cousin cat named Brown.
As he went on his merry way,
And sauntered out of town

He said, "My friends you must admit
That cat deserves a bow.
And if you'll take my word for it,
I'll tell you something now:

It doesn't matter if you're rich
Or poor or great or small;
It's the very nicest one which
Is considered best of all".

Roy A. Stoll

The Considerate Cat

A country cat came in to town
To see his city cousin.
That is, to see the one named Brown.
(He had at least a dozen).

Now cousin Brown was very rich,
Oh, very rich indeed,
For he controlled a fortune which
Was made in catnip seed.

He had a big apartment house,
A fancy car to drive,
And he ate only "imported mouse"
(And on them he did thrive).

For he was fat as any cat
Which I have ever seen.
And though it's true that he was fat,
He also kept quite clean.

He washed his face before each meal
And washed when he was through.
He knew how good it made him feel
(And surely you do too!)

The country cat was much impressed
With all that he had seen.
His cousin Brown was neatly dressed.
(If you know what I mean.).

He always kept his clothes so neat
They almost looked like new,
Clear from his hat down to his feet.
(Perhaps that's just like you).

And city cat said "Thank you, Sir",
And "Please" and also "Pardon".
For, just as if his manner were
A pretty flower garden,

He gave them tender care each day.
And I'm sure you will find,
If you're just as nice, folks will say
That you're the thoughtful kind.

The country cat enjoyed his stay
With cousin cat named Brown.
As he went on his merry way,
And sauntered out of town

He said, "My friends you must admit
That cat deserves a bow.
And if you'll take my word for it,
I'll tell you something now:

It doesn't matter if you're rich
Or poor or great or small;
It's the very nicest one which
Is considered best of all".

DAD'S
THOUGHTS
ON FAMILY

Hello, Lila Darling;

Don't need to refrigerate my love to keep it, for you have preserved it forever
with your many thoughtful ways. but I do want you to know that my love for you is
everywhere with you--even in the most out-of-the-way places. Thanks for being my
wife and, in doing so, bringing so much happiness into my heart.

                                                          Love,
                                                          Roy

Hello, Lila darling;

Don't need to refrigerate my love to keep it, for you have preserved it forever with your many thoughtful ways. But I do want you to know that my love for you is everywhere with you - - even in the most out-of-the-way places. Thanks for being my wife and, in doing so, bringing so much happiness into my heart.

Love,
Roy

                    Tell Me, Lila

Tell me, Lila -- Tell me, Love;
Is your heart so cold and still
That you cannot speak of love,
Or my heart with rapture fill?

Tell me, Lila -- Tell me, Mine:
Is your heart so still and cold
That you know not live divine,
Nor the lips by love made bold?

Must you fear the fond embrace,
The soft word spoken in your ear,
The radiance of a smiling face--
Or is it love alone you fear?

Tell Me, Lila

Tell me, Lila - - Tell me, Love:
Is your heart so cold and still
That you cannot speak of love,
Or my heart with rapture fill?

Tell me, Lila - - Tell me, Mine:
Is your heart so still and cold
That you know not love divine,
Nor the lips by love made bold?

Must you fear the fond embrace,
The soft word spoken in your ear,
The radiance of a smiling face - -
Or is it love alone you fear?

An Open Book

Each day is a page in my life
To share with Lila, mydarling wife:

Each year a chapter of love for you.
There's more to read when this one's through.

A continued story with chapter one
Recently finished, the second begun.

May it's thrills be as great as those before.
And each page hold a paragraph of happiness, or more.

The end isn't written to this story, my love.
For we wait each day for a page from above.

An Open Book

Each day is a page in my life
To share with Lila, my darling wife:

Each year a chapter of love for you,
There's more to read when this one's through.

A continued story with chapter one
Recently finished, the second begun.

May it's thrills be as great as those before.
And each page hold a paragraph of happiness, or more.

The end isn't written to this story, my love.
For we wait each day for a page from above.

    My sweet Lila; this poem may be full of mistakes and not quite fit what
I would want to convey. But this new life for us together is no mistake, and
I hope there may be many years for me to tell you what it means to me to be
able to share a home and life with you.

So welcome to our home, my house is truly yours. And while we may have no
garden walks to trod or flowers to pluck, our marriage should always be a
garden or real beauty with flowers of happiness growing abundantly there
in all seasons of our life.

May you find permanent and lasting happiness with me; my heart is really
here to please you and my love is yours, constant and abiding through the
years.

Welcome home, my lovely bride!

My sweet Lila; this poem may be full of mistakes and not quite fit what I would want to convey. But this new life for us together is no mistake, and I hope there may be many years for me to tell you what it means to me to be able to share a home and life with you.

So welcome to our home, my house is truly yours. And while we may have no garden walks to trod or flowers to pluck, our marriage should always be a garden or real beauty with flowers of happiness growing abundantly there in all seasons of our life.

May you find permanent and lasting happiness with me; my heart is really here to please you and my love is yours, constant and abiding through the years.

Welcome home, my lovely bride!

We're expecting a baby, my wife and I,
And counting the days as time goes by.
We're happy about the whole affair
And planning the clothes our child will wear.
We pleasantly heed the advice of mothers,
And courteously listen to that of others.
We question some things that we've been told,
And patiently rehear the old tales unfold.
We readily answer most questions for you
That concern health, home, and parenthood view.
With restraint we demur to discuss any name
We've chosen. And we admit to the same
In decision of sex; whether girl or boy
Is immaterial to us: Either will bring joy
That's boundless, we're sure. With open arms
We await you, dear baby, with all your charms.

We're expecting a baby, my wife and I,
And counting the days as time goes by.
We're happy about the whole affair
And planning the clothes our child will wear.
We pleasantly heed the advice of mothers,
And courteously listen to that of others.
We question some things that we've been told,
And patiently rehear the old tales unfold.
We readily answer most questions for you
That concern health, home, and parenthood view.
With restraint we demur to discuss any name
We've chosen. And we admit to the same
In decision of sex; whether girl or boy
Is immaterial to us: Either will bring joy
That's boundless, we're sure. With open arms
We await you, dear baby, with all your charms.

                              Waiting

While I am waiting on the doctor, stork, and baby
I'll have time to sit and cogitate (well, maybe).
Why do all prospective fathers look so harried?
Surely they contemplated this when they got married.
Some will try to fool you (but only look the clown)
Like that one calmly reading - a book held upside down.
That's twenty times he's neatly combed his hair,
And that one continually adjusts a tie that isn't there.
With each and every wail that penetrates the room.
Each man jumps up as summoned by the Voice of Doom.
But I've been here before and sit nonchalantly by --
And pare my nails (the dirt thattwice escaped my eye)
And watch amusedly the expectant fathers caper,
And chew my gum (Oops.' I forgot to remove the paper!)

Waiting

While I am waiting on the doctor, stork, and baby
I'll have time to sit and cogitate (well, maybe).
Why do all prospective fathers look so harried?
Surely they contemplated this when they got married.
Some will try to fool you (but only look the clown)
Like that one calmly reading – a book held upside down.
That's twenty times he's neatly combed his hair,
And that one continually adjusts a tie that isn't there.
With each and every wail that penetrates the room.
Each man jumps up as summoned by the Voice of Doom.
But I've been here before and sit nonchalantly by - -
And pare my nails (the dirt that twice escaped my eye)
And watch amusedly the expectant fathers caper,
And chew my gum (Oops! I forgot to remove the paper!)

A Baby's Thoughts

I wonder why it is -- don't you?
That, no matter who they are,
Folks look down and gurgle and coo
And say, "My, what a sweet baby you are"
Gee, doesn't he favor his mother",
Or, "Gosh, but she looks like her Dad".
"Now isn't that the nose of Dad's brother";
"Why, those are the eyes that Grandmother had".
But haven't you noticed or wouldn't you guess
That when I'm cross and when I squall,
No one's there to claim or confess
That I've inherited his traits at all.

A Baby's Thoughts

I wonder why it is - - don't you?
That, no matter who they are,
Folks look down and gurgle and coo
And say, "My, what a sweet baby you are".
"Gee, doesn't he favor his mother",
Or "Gosh, but she looks like her Dad".
"Now isn't that the nose of Dad's brother.";
"Why, those are the eyes that Grandmother had".
But haven't you noticed or wouldn't you guess
That when I'm cross and when I squall,
No one's there to claim or confess
That I've inherited his traits at all.

                    Ode to a Two Months Old Baby

Oh, you who are so fine and fair;
You of satin skin and silken hair;
You of fleeting smile and ready grin;
Of chubby arms and double chin;
You may not have your mother's face
Nor daddy's features bear a trace.
You may not have our ears or eyes,
But it should come as no surprise
That you have captured and confine
My heart in yours, Oh, Baby, Mine.

Ode to a Two Months Old Baby

Oh, you who are so fine and fair;
You of satin skin and silken hair;
You of fleeting smile and ready grin;
Of chubby arms and double chin;
You may not have your mother's face
Nor of daddy's features bear a trace,
You may not have our ears or eyes,
But it should come as no surprise
That you have captured and confine
My heart in yours, Oh, Baby, Mine.

I Like, I Love

I like your little dimple and
I love to hold your hand.
Its nice to stroke your hair
And say how much I care.
Its fun to kiss you and
Tell you that you're grand.
Its great to hold you near
And whisper in your ear.
I want you in my arms,
To tell you of your charms
And your lovely lips to kiss.
But most of all it's this
I'll always want to do:
Give all my love to you.

Roy H. Stoller

I Like, I Love

I like your little dimple and
I love to hold your hand.
Its nice to stroke your hair
And say how much I care.
Its fun to kiss you and
Tell you that you're grand.
Its great to hold you near
And whisper in your ear.
I want you in my arms,
To tell you of your charms
And your lovely lips to kiss.
But most of all it's this
I'll always want to do:
Give all my love to you.

Sixteen months we've been married, now;
Sixteen months since our wedding vow.
Sixteen months of wedded bliss
Since we shared the marriage kiss.
Sixteen months that seem so few,
Each one filled with something new:
Of love and wonder --you, delight --
That opened to us our wedding night.
Sixteen months, you have given me,
Of passion, tenderness and purity.
Sixteen months, and the added joy
of a precious son -- a baby boy.
The rest of the years that passeth by
May not be as perfect, but,Dear, I'll try!

Sixteen months we've been married, now;
Sixteen months since our wedding vow.
Sixteen months of wedded bliss
Since we shared the marriage kiss.
Sixteen months that seem so few,
Each one filled with something new:
Of love and wonder - - you, delight - -
That opened to us our wedding night.
Sixteen months, you have given me,
Of passion, tenderness and purity.
Sixteen months, and the added joy
of a precious son - - a baby boy.
The rest of the years that passeth by
May not be as perfect, but, Dear, I'll try!

Within my heart, I must confess,
There's a deeper well of tenderness
Than e'er before I did possess
Since you came to us, no less,
With winning ways and sparkling eyes;
With dimpled cheeks and plaintive cries,
With mough and face that shows surprise
As your new world before you lies.

You've opened up for us to see
A door to faith and purity
That ne'er before was known to me,
And strength to face eternity.

In us I trust that you will find
A loving heart, and peace of mind
To know that we are firm but kind.
For through such strength and love we bind
The family ties. And you will know,
As you learn and as you grow,
As years come and as they go,
That life is thus and life is so.

For the faith and love we hold,
From our youth until we're old,
Is fashioned from the selfsame mold
From which our parents' did unfold.

So to our life (with this in view)
You've added something that is new.
And if this is so, then it will do
For us to give it back to you.

Within my heart, I must confess,
There's a deeper well of tenderness
Than e'er before I did possess
Since you came to us, no less,
With winning ways and sparkling eyes;
With dimpled cheeks and plaintive cries,
With mouth and face that shows surprise
As your new world before you lies.

You've opened up for us to see
A door to faith and purity
That ne'er before was known to me,
And strength to face eternity.

In us I trust that you will find
A loving heart, and peace of mind
To know that we are firm but kind.
For through such strength and love we bind
The family ties. And you will know,
As you learn and as you grow,
As years come and as they go,
That life is thus and life is so.

For the faith and love we hold,
From our youth until we're old.
Is fashioned from the selfsame mold
From which our parents did unfold.

So to our life (with this in view)
You've added something that is new.
And if this is so, then it will do
For us to give it back to you.

No scanned poem available

If you'd open the door & look within
you'd see a home like many that's been.
But if you'd tarry a while and step inside,
you'd sense the reasons of a father's pride.

There's a wife who shares his fondest dreams
and understands his every word, it seems,
by doing or saying just the right thing
and making him glad she's wearing his ring.

There are children to share in the greatest of joys:
* one curly-haired girl and 2 older boys. *
They pounce on their Dad with great shouts of glee
and he's proud of his wife and these precious three.

There is news to be told and adventures to share
and we know in our hearts that each one of us care
what Daddy can tell that seems worth while,
what happened at home are tails to beguile.

Mom added at a later date:

For in our home God is supreme, His presence is
reflected, In love & understanding, & each persons
rights respected.

MISCELLANEOUS BIRTHDAY NOTES

May the nineteenth day of January,
With its gifts of every hue,
Be a day you long remember
Of the life we're passing through.
May your eighteenth birthday
Bring you joy you've never known,
That will fill your heart with gladness
And a love you'll call your own;
One that bids you answer, Dear,
With the love that's in your heart.
May it ever be a blessing and
A bond we'll never part.
Come my Love and love confess;
Give me your answer--answer, "Yes".

May the nineteenth day of January,
With its gifts of every hue,
Be a day you long remember
Of the life we're passing through.
May your eighteenth birthday
Bring you joy you've never known,
That will fill your heart with gladness
And a love you'll call your own;
One that bids you answer, Dear,
With the love that's in your heart.
May it ever be a blessing and
A bond we'll never part.
Come my Love and love confess;
Give me your answer - - answer, "Yes".

To a Young Bride on Her Birthday

Your Birthday's come now twenty times
And here's -- Yes, count them -- twenty dimes.
Seven months as wife you've spent --
With God's approval, parents' consent.
To these now add five months more
(Third finger, left hand, a diamond wore).
And these traits are the other eight:
Patience for all the times I'm late;
Personal habits that are so neat;
Manners (and smile) that are sweet;
Considerateness for my taste in foods;
Understanding, and tolerance of moods.
Cooperation in all that we do.
Kindness, always, is another virtue.
And more you've shown --by twenty times --
But I didn't have that many dimes.'

Second Gift

The best things come in pairs,
My love.
I hope these fit yours "like
a glove."

Number Three

It may be that you <u>stole</u> my heart
That this gift came to mind
And if it does not "<u>Cape</u>"*you warm
It's the best that I could find.

*Apologies to the Irish.

To a Young Bride on Her Birthday

Your Birthday's come now twenty times
And here's - - Yes, count them - - twenty dimes.
Seven months as wife you've spent - -
With God's approval, parent's consent.
To these now add five months more
(Third finger, left hand, a diamond wore).
And these traits are the other eight:
Patience for all the times I'm late;
Personal habits that are so neat;
Manners (and smile) that are sweet.
Considerateness for my taste in foods;
Understanding, and tolerance of moods.
Cooperation in all that we do.
Kindness, always, is another virtue.
And more you've shown - - by twenty times - -
But I didn't have that many dimes.

———

Second Gift

The best things come in pairs,
My love.
I hope these fit yours "like
a glove."

———

Number Three

It may be that you <u>stole</u> my heart
That this gift came to mind
And if it does not "<u>Cape</u>"* you warm
It's the best that I could find.

*Apologies to the Irish.

I'm empty now as you will see,
But soon will be inside of me:
Compact, pencil, roll of film;
Lipstick, pen, chewing gum;
Paper, pictures, emery board;
Thread, needles, darning gourd;
Thimble, tweezers, bobby pins;
Nail file, clippers, aspirin tins;
Earrings, bills, address book;
Mirror for a hasty look;
Comb and coins, ring of keys;
And other things to add to these.

I'm empty now as you will see,
But soon will be inside of me:
Compact, pencil, roll of tums;
Lipstick, pen, chewing gum;
Paper, pictures, emery board;
Thread, needles, darning gourd;
Thimble, kleenex, bobby pins;
Nail file, clippers, aspirin tins;
Earrings, bills, address book;
Mirror for a hasty look;
Comb and coins, ring of keys;
And other things to add to these.

UNTITLED
POEMS

A bird or just a feather,
Flowers or piece of heather,
Fish net or strand of rope,
"Fruit stand or cake of soap;
Made of straw — two feet wide;
Cotton braid — one each side;
No two alike: "who is that?
Got her nerve, the copy cat"!;
Back of head, over one eye;
Oil derrick in the sky;
Need you ask, "what is that?"
All the same — woman's hat!

A bird or just a feather,
Flower or piece of heather,
Fish net or strand of rope,
Fruit stand or cake of soap;
Made of straw – two feet wide;
Cotton tails – one each side;
Two alike: "Who is that?
Got her nerve, the copy cat"!;
Back of head, over one eye;
Oil derrick in the sky;
Need you ask, "What is that?"
All the same – woman's hat!

The lack of words, may I lament,
Stays the power of bright comment.
Without the knowledge of the word,
Lips are sealed, no wisdom heard.
Words are the tools of man's power
That build for him a famed bower.
Words are the windows of the world;
Through them life's beauty is unfurled.
If you want to understand,
Or attention of the throng command--
If you would seek an honored name,
Or any other claim to fame --
Know good diction; use it, too;
That's the thing for you to do.

The lack of words, may I lament,
Stays the power of bright comment.
Without the knowledge of the word,
Lips are sealed, no wisdom heard.
Words are the tools of man's power
That build for him a famed bower.
Words are the windows of the world;
Through them life's beauty is unfurled.
If you want to understand,
Or attention of the throng command - -
If you would seek an honored name,
Or any other claim to fame - -
Know good diction; use it, too;
That's the thing for you to do.

If tears must flow, then be it so;
They cleanse the soul, and make one whole.
The feeling of our deepest love,
Ne'er stops a tear when it is here,
From welling out.
As tear drops flow, our love will grow.
Tears water the soils from which love toils
And birds will flit in gardens of it,
Gathering nectar of the blossoms of love
Just coming out.

If tears must flow, then be it so;
They cleanse the soul, and make one whole.
The feeling of our deepest love,
Ne'er stops a tear when it is here,
From welling out.
As tear drops flow, our love will grow.
Tears water the soils from which love toils.
And birds will flit in gardens of it,
Gathering nectar of the blossoms of Love
Just coming out.

Sitting here in my lonely room --
The only company, silence and gloom --
Reminiscing and living again
The days of "remember when",
I ponder on my foolish deeds
Showing like obnoxious weeds
In an unkempt garden.

Was it an inherent trait
When I blamed the broken gate
On my unfortunate brother?
Or was it just another
Sowing of those ugly weeds,
Instead of planting flower seeds
In my unkempt garden?

Sitting here in my lonely room - -
The only company, silence and gloom - -
Reminiscing and living again
The days of "remember when",
I ponder on my foolish deeds
Showing like obnoxious weeds
In an unkempt garden.

Was it an inherent trait
When I blamed the broken gate
On my unfortunate brother?
Or was it just another
Sowing of those ugly weeds,
Instead of planting flower seeds
In my unkempt garden?

www.ingramcontent.com/pod-product-compliance
Lightning Source LLC
Chambersburg PA
CBHW071329130726
47996CB00002B/681

CULTŪRA